Editor
Eric Migliaccio

Managing Editor
Ina Massler Levin, M.A.

Editor-in-Chief
Sharon Coan, M.S. Ed.

Illustrator
Bruce Hedges

Cover Artist
Brenda DiAntonis

Art Coordinator
Kevin Barnes

Art Director
CJae Froshay

Imaging
Rosa C. See
James Edward Grace

Product Manager
Phil Garcia

Publisher
Mary D. Smith, M.S. Ed.

Correlations to the Common Core State Standards can be found at *http://www.teachercreated.com/standards/*.

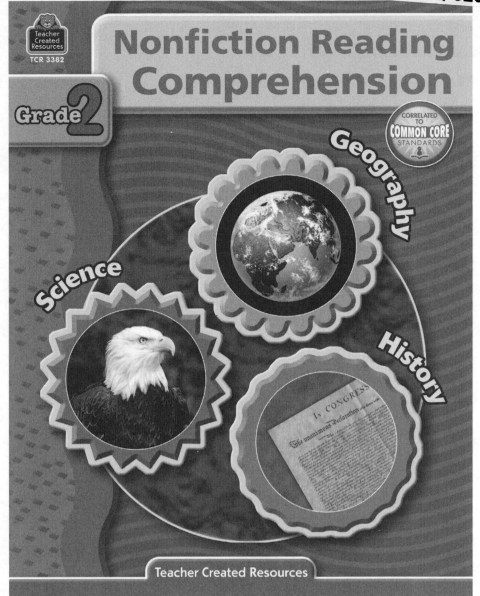

Nonfiction Reading Comprehension

Grade 2

Science • Geography • History

Teacher Created Resources

Author

Debra J. Housel, M.S. Ed.

Teacher Created Resources, Inc.
6421 Industry Way
Westminster, CA 92683
www.teachercreated.com

ISBN: 978-0-7439-3382-7

©2002 Teacher Created Resources, Inc.
Reprinted, 2013
Made in U.S.A.

Table of Contents

Introduction

Comprehension is the primary goal of any reading task. Students who comprehend expository text will have more opportunities in life, as well as better test performance. Through the use of nonfiction passages followed by exercises that require vital reading and thinking skills, *Nonfiction Reading Comprehension* will help you to develop confident readers and promote the foundation comprehension skills necessary for a lifetime of learning.

Each passage in *Nonfiction Reading Comprehension* covers a grade-level-appropriate curriculum topic in science, geography, or history. The activities are time-efficient, allowing students to practice these skills often. To yield the best results, such practice must begin as soon as the majority of your students can read at the 2.0 level.

✦ Essential Comprehension Skills

The questions following each passage in *Nonfiction Reading Comprehension* always appear in the same order and cover seven vital skills:

✧ Locating facts

Questions based on exactly what the text states (who, what, when, where, why, and how many)

✧ Identifying sequence

Questions based on chronological order (what happened first, last, and in between)

✧ Noting conditions

Questions that ask students to identify similarities and differences, as well as cause-and-effect relationships

✧ Understanding vocabulary in context

Questions based on the ability to infer word meaning from the syntax and semantics of the surrounding text, as well as the ability to recognize known synonyms and antonyms for a newly encountered word

✧ Making inferences

Questions that require students to evaluate, to make decisions, and to draw logical conclusions

✧ Integrating knowledge

Questions that ask readers to draw upon their visualization skills combined with prior knowledge (These questions reinforce the crucial skill of picturing the text.)

✧ Supporting an answer

A short-answer question at the end of each passage that helps students to personalize knowledge, state an opinion, and support it

Meeting Standards and Benchmarks

Every passage in *Nonfiction Reading Comprehension* and its comprehension questions cover one or more language arts standards.*

Reading	Writing
• Understands how print is organized and read	• Uses frequently used words to express basic ideas
• Uses schema to understand new information	• Write complete, simple sentences
• Integrates new information into personal knowledge base	• Uses nouns, verbs, adjectives, and pronouns to make writing diverse and interesting
• Uses context clues to decode unknown words	• Writes in a logical sequence
• Self-monitors reading and takes action to increase understanding (self-corrects, re-reads if necessary)	• Follows conventions of capitalization, spelling, and punctuation appropriate for grade level
• Makes and revises predictions about text	• States an opinion and supports it in writing
• Visualizes what is read in text	
• Understands the main idea of nonfiction text	
• Reflects on what has been read and develops ideas, opinions, and personal responses	

The specific McREL content area standard and benchmark for each passage appears in a box at the top of each passage. Used with permission from McREL. (Copyright 2000 McREL, Mid-continent Research for Education and Learning. Telephone: 303-337-0990. Website: www.mcrel.org). Visit *http://www.teachercreated.com/standards/* for correlations to the Common Core State Standards.

✚ Readability

All of the passages have a 2.0–2.9 reading level based on the Flesch-Kincaid Readability Formula. This formula, built into Microsoft Word, determines a readability level by calculating the number of words, syllables, and sentences. Although content area terms can be challenging, students can handle difficult words within the context given. The passages are presented in order of increasing difficulty within each content area.

✚ Preparing Students to Read Nonfiction Text

Prepare your students to read the passages in *Nonfiction Reading Comprehension* by reading aloud a short selection *from another source* each day. Reading expository text aloud is critical to developing your students' ability to read it themselves. Since making predictions is important to understanding nonfiction, read the beginning of a passage, then stop and ask them to predict what might occur next. Do this at several points throughout your reading of the text. Talking about nonfiction concepts is also very important. Remember, however, that discussion can never replace reading aloud because people rarely use the vocabulary and complex sentence structures of written language when they speak.

* Kendall, John S. and Robert J. Marzano (1997) *Content Knowledge: A Compendium of Standards and Benchmarks for K–12 Education, 2nd Ed.* Aurora, CO. McREL. Used by permission of McREL.

How to Use this Book

If you have some students who cannot read the articles independently, allow them to read with a partner, then work through the comprehension questions alone. As soon as possible, move to having all students practice reading and answering the questions independently.

✛ Multiple-Choice Questions

Do the first two passages and related questions (pages 8–11) with the whole class. These passages have the most challenging reading level (2.9) because you will do them together. Demonstrate your own cognitive process by thinking aloud about how to figure out an answer. This means that you essentially tell your students your thoughts as they come to you. Let's say that this is a passage your class has read:

Once 100,000 grizzly bears lived in the U.S. Today there are only 1,000. But 30 years ago there were even fewer bears. So in 1975 a law was passed to keep people from hurting the bears or their homes. Now there are more bears than in 1975. Most of them live in Yellowstone National Park. But sometimes the bears leave the park. They kill cows or sheep. Some people are afraid. They want to shoot any bear that's outside the park. But others say that there are already too few bears. They do not want the law changed.

Following the reading, one of the questions is: "In Yellowstone National park, grizzly bears a) roam free, b) live in cages, or c) get caught in traps." Tell the students all your thoughts as they occur to you: "Well, the article said that the bears sometimes leave the park, so they must not be in cages. So I'll get rid of that choice. That leaves me with the choices 'roam free' or 'get caught in traps.' Let me look back at the article and see what it says about traps." (Refer back to article.) "I don't see anything about traps in the passage. And I did see that it says that there is a law to keep the bears safe. That means they're safe from traps, which are dangerous. So I'm going to select '(a) roam free.'"

The fourth question is always about vocabulary. Teach students to substitute the word choices into the sentence in the passage where the vocabulary term is found. For each choice they should ask, "Does this make sense?" This will help them to make the best choice. If the question asks for an antonym, have them do the substitution looking for the one that makes it the most false.

Teach students to look for the key words in a response or question and search for those specific words in the text. Explain that they may need to look for synonyms for the key words. When you go over the practice passages, ask your students to show where they found the correct response *in the text*.

How to Use this Book *(cont.)*

✤ Short-Answer Questions

The short-answer question for each passage is an opinion statement with no definitive right answer. The student makes a statement and explains it. While there is no correct response, it is critical to show them how to support their opinions using facts and logic. Show them a format for response: "I think _____ because _____. For example: I think that whales should not be kept at sea parks because they are wild animals and don't want to be there. They want to be in the ocean with their friends." *Do not award credit unless the student adequately supports his or her conclusion.* Before passing back the practice papers, make note of students with opposing opinions or different viewpoints. Then during the discussion call on each of these students to read his or her short answer response to the class. (If all your students drew the same conclusion or had the same opinion, state another view yourself.)

For the most effective practice sessions, follow these steps:

- Have students read the text silently and answer the questions.

- Collect all the papers to score them.

- Return the papers to the students and discuss how they determined their answers.

- Point out how students had to use their background knowledge to answer certain questions.

- Call on at least two students with different viewpoints to read and discuss their responses to the short-answer question.

- Have your students complete the achievement bar graph on page 7, showing how many questions they answered correctly for each practice passage. Seeing their scores improve or stay consistently high over time will provide encouragement and motivation.

Scoring the Passages

Since the passages are meant as skill builders, do not include the passage scores in students' class grades. With the students, use the "number correct" approach to scoring the practice passages, especially since this coincides with the student achievement graph on page 7. However, for your own records and to share with the parents, you may want to keep a track of numeric scores for each student. If you choose to do this, do not write the numeric score on the paper. To generate a numeric score, follow these guidelines:

Multiple-choice questions (6)	15 points each	90 points
Short-answer questions (1)	10 points	10 points
Total		**100 points**

✤ Practice Makes Perfect

The more your students practice, the more competent and confident they will become. Plan to have your class do every exercise in *Nonfiction Reading Comprehension Practice*. If you do so, you'll be pleased with your students' improved comprehension of *any* expository text—within your classroom and beyond its walls.

Achievement Graph

Number Correct

Passage	1	2	3	4	5	6	7
"The White House"	✓	✗	✓	✓	✓	✗	✓
"Electricity on the Move"	✓	✗	✓	✓	✓	✓	✓
"Day and Night"							
"The American Toad Hops Again"							
"Animal Instincts"							
"Busy as a Bee"							
"The Platypus"							
"The Rock Cycle"							
"Getting Around"							
"Leafy Forests"							
"Sharing Ideas"							
"Grasslands"							
"Saving the Calvaria Trees"							
"City or Suburb?"							
"Early American Colonies"							
"She Made the First American Flag"							
"The American Bald Eagle"							
"The Statue That Stands for Freedom"							
"Presidents' Day"							
"Memorial Day"							

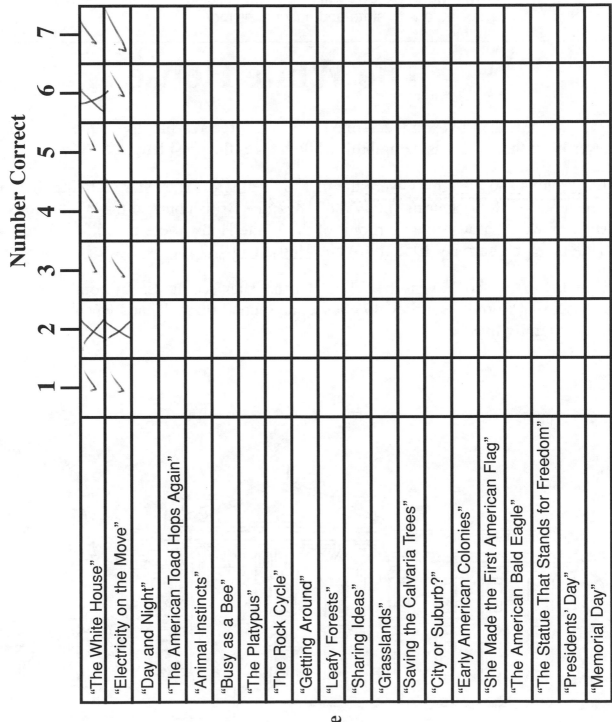

Geography Standard: Understands how democratic values came to be and how they have been exemplified by people, events, and symbols

Benchmark: Knows why important buildings, statues, and monuments are associated with state and national history

The White House

The U.S. president lives in the White House. George Washington is the only one who never lived there. It was being built while he was the president.

① Strategy:

John Adams and his family were the first to live there. They started living there in November of 1800. During the War of 1812, the British burned the White House. After America won that war, the 62 rooms of the White House were **rebuilt**. Later it was made much bigger. By 1952 the White House had 132 rooms.

Each day many people visit the White House. They see the East Room. They see the State Dining Room. But they do not see the second floor. That's where today's leader and his family live.

71% C

The White House

Comprehension Questions

Fill in the circle next to the best answer.

1. **Which American president never lived in the White House?**

    ⓐ George Washington

    ⓑ John Adams

    ⓒ Abe Lincoln

2. **What happened last?**

    ⓐ John Adams lived in the White House.

    ⓑ The White House had 132 rooms.

    ⓒ The White House burned.

3. **England's queen lives in Windsor Palace, which has 1,000 rooms. Compared to it, our White House is**

    ⓐ the same size.

    ⓑ bigger.

    ⓒ smaller.

4. **The word *rebuilt* means**

    ⓐ built again.

    ⓑ torn down.

    ⓒ nailed together.

5. **Why don't people get to see the White House's second floor?**

    ⓐ because there are no stairs to reach it

    ⓑ because the president and his family need a place to be alone

    ⓒ because it was ruined by the fire

6. **Picture the White House when it was on fire. What *don't* you see?**

    ⓐ smoke

    ⓑ flames

    ⓒ a fire truck

7. **Would you like to visit the White House? Explain.**

    I would because I think it is
    nice. And want to live in there.

6/20/18

Geography Standard: Understands energy types, sources, and conversions and their relationship to heat and temperature

Benchmark: Knows that electricity in circuits can produce light, heat, sound, and magnetic effects

Electricity on the Move

Electricity is important. We need it to turn on lights. We use it to toast bread. We need it for our computers. We use it to watch TV. When you plug anything in, you use electricity.

Electricity is made in a power plant. Wires bring electricity to your home. Some things let electricity pass through them. Metal does this. That's why electric wires are metal. Other things stop electricity. Electricity cannot pass through them. Glass does this. Plastic and rubber do, too. Electric wires have covers of rubber or plastic to keep the electricity from leaving the wire.

Lightning is natural electricity that starts in a cloud. It can go to another cloud or to the ground. Since electricity is so **powerful**, you must take care. Never touch wires on the ground. And when there is a storm, come inside.

86% B

Electricity on the Move

Comprehension Questions

Fill in the circle next to the best answer.

1. **What do we call the kind of electricity found in nature?**
   - (a) static
   - (b) lightning
   - (c) power

2. **What happens first?**
   - (a) Electricity flows through wires.
   - (b) Electricity turns on your lamp.
   - (c) Electricity is made at a power plant.

3. **An electric wire has a torn cover. Now the electricity may**
   - (a) not stay inside of the wire.
   - (b) become more powerful.
   - (c) shut it off.

4. **The word *powerful* means**
   - (a) hard.
   - (b) angry.
   - (c) strong.

5. **Before electricity, what did people use for light in their homes?**
   - (a) candles
   - (b) matches
   - (c) lasers

6. **Picture yourself at home after the electricity has gone out. What can you still use?**
   - (a) the VCR
   - (b) a flashlight
   - (c) the microwave

7. **What is your favorite thing that runs on electricity? Explain.**

   My favorite is the TV because
   I can watch cartoons.

Science Standard: Understands essential ideas about the composition and structure of the universe and the Earth's place in it

Benchmark: Knows the basic patterns of the sun and moon

Day and Night

Every day the sun comes up. And every day the sun goes down. Why?

The sun doesn't move around the Earth. The Earth spins as it goes around the sun. The part of the Earth facing the sun has day. The part of the Earth facing away from the sun has night. It takes the Earth 24 hours, or one day, to spin around once.

Sometimes we see the moon at night. Sometimes we see it in the day, too. The moon is always in the sky. But the sun is so bright we **usually** can't see the moon during the day. The moon goes around the Earth. It takes the moon 27.3 days to go around once.

The Earth is not just spinning. It is also following a path around the sun. It takes the Earth one year to go all the way around the sun. During that time it has different seasons. The seasons are based on where Earth is on its path around the sun.

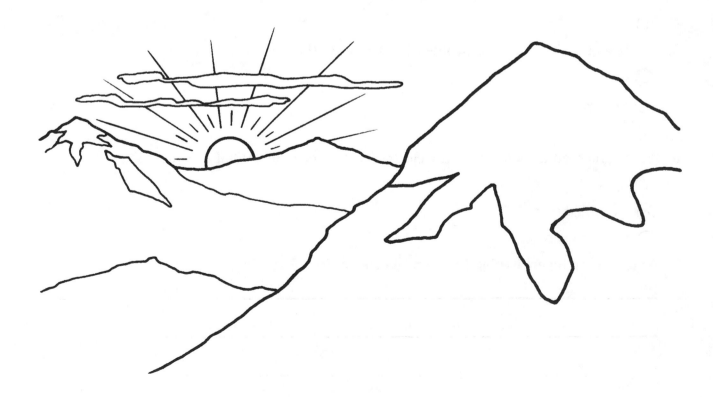

Day and Night

Comprehension Questions

Fill in the circle next to the best answer.

1. **Which does *not* move around another object?**

   ⓐ the Earth

   ⓑ the moon

   ⓒ the sun

2. **What season comes after winter?**

   ⓐ spring

   ⓑ fall

   ⓒ summer

3. **Because the Earth is always spinning, part of the planet is always**

   ⓐ wet.

   ⓑ in the dark.

   ⓒ cold.

4. **The word *usually* means**

   ⓐ almost never.

   ⓑ sometimes.

   ⓒ most of the time.

5. **What happens every 27.3 days?**

   ⓐ The moon goes around the Earth once.

   ⓑ The moon goes around the sun once.

   ⓒ A week passes.

6. **Picture a sunset. What is happening on the other side of the world?**

   ⓐ The sun and moon are seen together.

   ⓑ The sun is rising.

   ⓒ The moon comes out.

7. **Which do you like better: day or night? Explain.**

   _____

   _____

   _____

Science Standard: Understands how species depend on one another and on the environment for survival

Benchmark: Knows that living things are found almost everywhere in the world and that distinct environments support the life of different types of plants and animals

The American Toad Hops Again

You may see American toads in a park or your yard. But they didn't start out there. They hatched from eggs in a pond. They stayed tadpoles for ten days. Toad tadpoles are darker and smaller than frog tadpoles. Like fish, tadpoles have gills. As their limbs grow and their tail **shrinks**, they get lungs. Then they must get out of the water or drown. When they leave the pond, they are tiny toads.

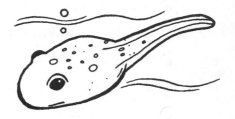

Toads catch bugs with their tongues and swallow them. Although baby toads are tiny, no toad ever thinks one is a bug. Toads can see a glow on another toad's skin. That way they don't eat each other. The first summer a toad sheds its skin every three days. While it sleeps during its first winter, its skin gets bumpy.

Toads can live up to 30 years. They can get really big. But snakes and birds eat most of them before that. If they live to be three years old, they go to a pond. There they lay eggs that will hatch into more tadpoles.

The American Toad Hops Again

Comprehension Questions

Fill in the circle next to the best answer.

1. **What age can a toad reach?**

   (a) 30 years old

   (b) 3 years old

   (c) 30 months old

2. **What happens last?**

   (a) The tadpole has gills.

   (b) The tadpole hatches from an egg.

   (c) The tadpole has lungs.

3. **If a toad sees a snake, the toad will**

   (a) eat the snake.

   (b) try to get away from it.

   (c) not care.

4. **The word *shrinks* means**

   (a) breaks.

   (b) gets bigger.

   (c) gets smaller.

5. **Why do toads wait three years before laying eggs?**

   (a) They need to grow up.

   (b) They need to eat bugs.

   (c) They need to sleep through the winter.

6. **Picture a toad catching food. What is it grabbing?**

   (a) a snail

   (b) a baby toad

   (c) a fly

7. **Do you like toads? Explain.**

   _____

   _____

   _____

Science Standard: Understands how species depend on one another and on the environment for survival

Benchmark: Knows that the behavior of individual organisms is influenced by internal cues and external cues and that humans and other organisms have senses that help them to detect these cues

Animal Instincts

If you buy a pet mouse, it will hide when you first put your hand in its cage. Or it may bite you. The little animal does not know you yet. It is afraid. When any animal is scared, it fights or runs away. This instinct is called "fight or flight." All animals and people have this instinct. You are born with it. No one teaches it to you.

Hibernating is an instinct for many animals where there are cold winters. When it gets cold, they hibernate. They go into a deep sleep for months. Their breathing slows down. Their hearts beat slowly. Frogs, bears, and turtles hibernate.

Other animals have an instinct to **migrate**. Birds and butterflies fly south in late fall. They stay there until spring. Then they fly back. Instinct tells them when it is time to go south. It also tells them when it is time to return north.

Animal Instincts

Comprehension Questions

Fill in the circle next to the best answer.

1. **What does "fight or flight" mean?**

   ⓐ any animal will fly if it's afraid

   ⓑ any animal will bite if it's afraid

   ⓒ any animal will fight or try to get away if it's afraid

2. **What came first?**

   ⓐ The birds go south.

   ⓑ The weather turns colder.

   ⓒ The birds go north.

3. **Why do birds fly north in the spring?**

   ⓐ The weather is getting warmer in the north.

   ⓑ Other birds chase them away.

   ⓒ They can't find food where they are.

4. **The word *migrate* means**

   ⓐ to come home.

   ⓑ to fly.

   ⓒ to go to a different place.

5. **How does hibernation help an animal?**

   ⓐ It lets the animal lose weight.

   ⓑ It lets the animal sleep when food is hard to find.

   ⓒ It keeps the animal away from things that would eat it.

6. **Picture a frog sitting near a pond. As you get closer, the frog jumps into the water. What instinct made it do this?**

   ⓐ fight or flight

   ⓑ migrating

   ⓒ hibernating

7. **If you were an animal, would you rather hibernate or migrate for the winter? Explain.**

   _____

   _____

   _____

Science Standard: Understands how species depend on one another and on the environment for survival

Benchmark: Knows that living things are found almost everywhere in the world and that distinct environments support the life of different types of plants and animals

Busy as a Bee

Bees keep busy all year. In spring the worker bees go out to find flowers. At each flower they get pollen or nectar. Then they go back to the hive. They turn the nectar into honey. They store the pollen to eat later.

The queen lays all of the eggs. But the worker bees do all of the work. Some worker bees feed the baby bees. They give them a mix of honey and pollen called beebread. They build the honeycomb and guard the hive. Other worker bees take care of the queen.

In the fall, worker bees use water and plant sap to fix cracks in the hive. Then the worker bees gather around their queen and move their wings **rapidly**. They keep her warm.

The bees help us. By going from plant to plant, bees spread pollen. This makes some plants grow fruits and vegetables. Without bees, fewer fruits and vegetables would grow.

Busy as a Bee

Comprehension Questions

Fill in the circle next to the best answer.

1. **Which bees lay all the eggs?**

   ⓐ worker bees

   ⓑ queen bees

   ⓒ baby bees

2. **What happens last?**

   ⓐ The worker bees feed the baby bees.

   ⓑ The worker bees get pollen from flowers.

   ⓒ The worker bees make beebread.

3. **What happens after a bee visits the flowers on a cherry tree?**

   ⓐ The tree grows more roots.

   ⓑ The tree drops its leaves.

   ⓒ The tree grows cherries.

4. **The word *rapidly* means**

   ⓐ around.

   ⓑ slow.

   ⓒ fast.

5. **What do bees make that we sometimes eat?**

   ⓐ honey

   ⓑ pollen

   ⓒ beebread

6. **Picture a boy getting close to a beehive. Worker bees buzz all around him. What will probably happen next?**

   ⓐ The bees will fly away.

   ⓑ The bees will sting him.

   ⓒ The bees will give him honey.

7. **Beekeepers take care of bee hives. Do you think that you'd like to be a beekeeper when you grow up? Explain.**

   _____

   _____

   _____

Science Standard: Knows about the diversity and unity that characterize life

Benchmark: Knows that plants and animals have features that help them live in different environments

The Platypus

A platypus is a mammal that lives only in Australia. Their wide, flat tails and webbed feet make them good swimmers. They scoop up worms and shellfish from stream bottoms with their wide, flat snouts. They use the claws on their feet to walk and to dig dirt. They dig burrows along streams.

Unlike most mammals, the platypus lays eggs. The female uses grass and leaves to make a nest at the end of her burrow. Next, she blocks the burrow's opening with dirt. Then she lays two or three eggs. After ten days, the babies hatch. They drink her milk for four months.

Adult platypuses are small. They are less than two feet long (0.6 m) and weigh just 5 pounds (2.3 kg). Their thick brown fur makes them look bigger. Hunters used to kill them for their fur. But now it is **illegal** to kill a platypus.

The Platypus

Comprehension Questions

Fill in the circle next to the best answer.

1. You can figure out that the platypus cannot

    (a) fly.

    (b) walk.

    (c) dig.

2. What happens first?

    (a) The female blocks off the burrow.

    (b) The female lays eggs.

    (c) The female makes a nest.

3. What makes platypuses so different from most other mammals?

    (a) They live in Australia.

    (b) They lay eggs.

    (c) They are small.

4. The word *illegal* means

    (a) against the law.

    (b) a good idea.

    (c) too hard.

5. What do young platypuses share with all other mammal babies?

    (a) They hatch from eggs.

    (b) They can swim.

    (c) They drink milk from their mother.

6. Picture a platypus burrow. What does it look the most like?

    (a) a nest in a tree

    (b) a hole in the ground

    (c) a big cave in some rocks

7. Do you agree with the law that says no one can hunt platypuses? Explain.

_____

_____

_____

Science Standard: Understands basic Earth processes

Benchmark: Knows how features on the Earth's surface are constantly changed by a combination of slow and rapid processes

The Rock Cycle

Like the blankets on a bed, the Earth has rock layers in its crust. There are many layers. The top layers are the newest. The bottom ones are the oldest.

Rocks on the Earth's **surface** are always wearing away. Rain, ice, wind, and moving water make little pieces break off. These little pieces of rock are like dirt. They blow away or get carried away by water. When the pieces are dropped, they form a new layer. Later more rock pieces cover them. In this way, layer after layer builds up.

After a long time, heat and pressure squeeze the lowest layer. The rocks get hotter and hotter. They begin to change. Rocks way down inside of the Earth melt. Later they come back to the Earth's crust as lava.

The Rock Cycle

Comprehension Questions

Fill in the circle next to the best answer.

1. **When rocks are under great heat and pressure they**
   - (a) wear away.
   - (b) melt.
   - (c) form a new layer.

2. **Which rocks are the oldest?**
   - (a) the rocks in the layers near the Earth's crust
   - (b) the rocks near a volcano
   - (c) the rocks in the layers deep inside the Earth

3. **How do melted rocks return to Earth's crust?**
   - (a) when a volcano erupts
   - (b) when a tornado hits
   - (c) when too little rain falls

4. **Another word for the Earth's *surface* is**
   - (a) crust.
   - (b) lava.
   - (c) layers.

5. **The top rock layers**
   - (a) are always melting.
   - (b) have been there for the longest time.
   - (c) have been there the least amount of time.

6. **Picture the rocks in a desert. What is slowly wearing them down?**
   - (a) moving water
   - (b) wind
   - (c) ice

7. **What do you think is doing the most wearing away of the rocks in your area? Explain.**

   _____

   _____

   _____

Geography Standard: Understands the changes that occur in the meaning, use, distribution, and importance of resources

Benchmark: Understands the role that resources play in our daily lives (food and transportation)

Getting Around

Long ago, people had to walk to get where they wanted to go. Then someone tamed horses. People could go farther than ever before. They could go faster, too. After a while, someone made a wagon for a horse to pull. Then people could move big, heavy things.

Today we have many ways to move people and things around. There are cars, boats, planes, and trains. There are big trucks. These are all forms of **transportation**.

How do you get bananas from South America? They are put on a big ship or plane. When they get to the U.S., they are unloaded. Then they are put on a train. At the train station, a truck picks them up. The truck takes the bananas to your store. That's how you can get foods from around the world!

Getting Around

Comprehension Questions

Fill in the circle next to the best answer.

1. **What first gave people the chance to travel far away?**

   (a) People tamed horses.

   (b) The people learned how to walk.

   (c) Someone made a wagon.

2. **Just like bananas, coconuts grow in South America. What happens first?**

   (a) You buy coconuts.

   (b) Coconuts go by truck to the store.

   (c) Coconuts go by ship to the U.S.A.

3. **What happened as a result of horses pulling wagons?**

   (a) People could travel faster than ever before.

   (b) People could cut logs in a forest and move them to a nearby town where they were needed.

   (c) Bananas could get to the U.S.A. from South America.

4. ***Transportation* means**

   (a) carrying things in a wagon.

   (b) going to a seaport.

   (c) moving people or things from one place to another.

5. **What is the fastest way to travel today?**

   (a) by truck

   (b) by plane

   (c) by wagon

6. **Picture a family moving west in a covered wagon. What heavy thing are they carrying inside their wagon?**

   (a) a rocking chair

   (b) some cattle

   (c) a pirate's treasure chest

7. **What is your favorite way to travel—car, train, bus, plane, or some other way? Explain.**

   _____

   _____

   _____

Geography Standard: Understands the physical and human characteristics of place

Benchmark: Knows that places can be defined in terms of their predominant human and physical characteristics

Leafy Forests

Leafy forests grow in places that have four seasons. The trees in these forests are usually maple, beech, and oak. They must change each spring, summer, fall, and winter. Pine trees can grow there, too. But they do not change with the seasons.

The trees in leafy forests have buds each spring. In early summer the buds open into green leaves. Each fall all of these leaves change to red, yellow, or brown. Then they drop. The trees stand **bare** all winter long. The next spring they have buds again. They go through these changes year after year for many years.

Many of the leafy forests that once grew in America are gone. They were cut down. The land was cleared and used for farms. But these forests still cover parts of the eastern U.S. and land near the Great Lakes.

Leafy Forests

Comprehension Questions

Fill in the circle next to the best answer.

1. **Why have so many of the leafy forests been cut down?**

   ⓐ The trees were dead.

   ⓑ People don't like leafy trees.

   ⓒ Farmers needed the land.

2. **What happens last?**

   ⓐ The trees have green leaves.

   ⓑ The trees lose their leaves.

   ⓒ The trees have red, yellow, or brown leaves.

3. **How are leafy forests different from pine forests?**

   ⓐ Leafy trees change with the seasons.

   ⓑ Pine trees live a lot longer.

   ⓒ Leafy trees aren't as pretty as pines.

4. **The word *bare* means**

   ⓐ a furry animal.

   ⓑ not covered.

   ⓒ a kind of fruit.

5. **What kind of tree would *never* be found in a leafy forest?**

   ⓐ a beech tree

   ⓑ a pine tree

   ⓒ a palm tree

6. **Picture a leafy forest on a sunny day. What animals do you see there?**

   ⓐ a squirrel

   ⓑ a kangaroo

   ⓒ a polar bear

7. **Which do you like better: leafy trees or pine trees? Explain.**

   _____

   _____

   _____

Geography Standard: Understands the nature and complexity of Earth's cultural mosaics

Benchmark: Knows the basic components of culture (e.g., language)

Sharing Ideas

People have always had ideas. They wanted to share them. Cave people moved their hands. They pointed. They smiled. They cried. Over time, people began to speak. This let them share their thoughts more clearly.

The first people also made pictures on cave walls. These pictures showed how to hunt deer. Much later, people around the world started to write. Each group came up with a different way. The Egyptians used **hieroglyphs**. Each picture stood for a sound or word. People in parts of Asia made marks in clay. Chinese and Japanese people used a symbol for each word. Some of their words are shown below. This is how they write today.

We use an alphabet of 26 letters. We use these letters in different orders to make our words. Aren't you glad that you can talk and write? It's much easier than drawing and pointing!

| month | book | person | next |

Sharing Ideas

Comprehension Questions

Fill in the circle next to the best answer.

1. People in Asia used marks in clay for

- (a) drawing.
- (b) money.
- (c) writing.

2. What happened first?

- (a) People wrote.
- (b) People pointed.
- (c) People spoke.

3. Once you learn to read, you can

- (a) find out about many other people's ideas.
- (b) share your own ideas.
- (c) draw.

4. *Hieroglyphs* are

- (a) a kind of pen.
- (b) photos.
- (c) pictures that stand for sounds and words.

5. Which skill is the most helpful to you when you use the Internet?

- (a) drawing
- (b) reading
- (c) speaking

6. Picture early people making pictures on cave walls. What are they drawing with?

- (a) a pen
- (b) a pencil
- (c) a piece of coal

7. Do you think that using an alphabet is the best way to write? Explain.

_____

_____

_____

Geography Standard: Understands the physical and human characteristics of place

Benchmark: Knows that places can be defined in terms of their predominant human and physical characteristics

Grasslands

Earth has different kinds of land areas. Grasslands are one kind. Grasslands are found far from oceans and lakes. These areas are covered by grass and are often called plains. Few trees grow there. The ground is flat. There is little rain. America's grasslands are in the plains states.

Grasslands cover parts of Africa. Zebra and antelope live there. Buffalo used to live on the North American plains. Today sheep and cattle **graze** there. They share the land with rabbits, deer, foxes, and skunks.

Grasslands have hot summers and cold winters. Their dirt is filled with dead, rotting grass. This makes rich, black soil that grows plants well. So all over the world grasslands have been turned into farms. These farms grow corn, wheat, and oats. People call our plains states "The Breadbasket of the World." These states grow so much grain that there is enough to share with other countries.

Grasslands

Comprehension Questions

Fill in the circle next to the best answer.

1. **Most grasslands are**
   - ⓐ near lakes.
   - ⓑ flat.
   - ⓒ wet.

2. **What happened first?**
   - ⓐ Buffalo lived on the plains.
   - ⓑ People killed the buffalo.
   - ⓒ Cattle lived on the plains.

3. **A grassland is a little like a desert because both areas have**
   - ⓐ winters that are very cold.
   - ⓑ rich soil for growing plants.
   - ⓒ little rain.

4. **Another word for *graze* is**
   - ⓐ eat.
   - ⓑ plain.
   - ⓒ farm.

5. **What types of wild animals live in a grassland?**
   - ⓐ Ones that like cool summers.
   - ⓑ Ones that need mild winters.
   - ⓒ Ones that hide in or eat grass.

6. **Picture a grassland on a sunny day. What don't you see?**
   - ⓐ a barn
   - ⓑ pine trees
   - ⓒ a field of corn

7. **If you could be one of the animals that live in the grasslands, which one would you be? Why?**

   _____

   _____

   _____

Geography Standard: Understands how human actions modify the physical environment

Benchmark: Knows ways in which the physical environment is stressed by human activities

Saving the Calvaria Trees

People can cause animals and plants to die off. Long ago, dodo birds lived on just one island. They could not fly. People caught and ate the birds. They brought pigs to the island. The pigs ate the birds' eggs. By 1680 no dodo birds were left.

In 1980 people noticed that all of the calvaria trees were more than 300 years old. They could not get any new ones to grow. They didn't know what to do. Then scientists found out that the seeds must be eaten. They had to go through an animal's gut in order to **sprout**. After the dodo birds were gone, no other animals had eaten these seeds.

So people fed the seeds to turkeys. After the turkeys passed the seeds, they planted them. And it worked! The seeds grew. They started new trees.

Saving the Calvaria Trees

Comprehension Questions

Fill in the circle next to the best answer.

1. **In the article, what died?**

   ⓐ all calvaria trees

   ⓑ most pigs

   ⓒ all dodo birds

2. **What happened first?**

   ⓐ People found a new way to start calvaria trees.

   ⓑ People brought pigs to the island.

   ⓒ People noticed that all of the calvaria trees were very old.

3. **What happened after the dodo birds were gone?**

   ⓐ No new calvaria trees started to grow.

   ⓑ More calvaria trees grew than ever before.

   ⓒ All of the calvaria trees died.

4. **To *sprout* means**

   ⓐ to die.

   ⓑ to start growing.

   ⓒ to grow taller.

5. **How did turkeys save the calvaria trees?**

   ⓐ They ate the trees' seeds.

   ⓑ They spread the trees' seeds far and wide.

   ⓒ They kept the trees' seeds cold.

6. **Picture a dodo bird's nest from long ago. Where is it?**

   ⓐ up in a tree

   ⓑ inside a barn

   ⓒ on the ground

7. **Why do you think people were upset when they couldn't grow any new calvaria trees?**

   _____

   _____

   _____

Geography Standard: Understands the patterns of human settlement and their causes

Benchmark: Knows the similarities and differences in housing and land use in urban and suburban areas

City or Suburb?

Many people live in a city. Their homes are close together. Cities have businesses and factories, too. There are tall office buildings and lots of places to work. Often people who live in the suburbs have jobs in the city.

Suburbs are the areas around a city. They have lots of houses. These homes have more space between them. The yards are bigger. Suburbs have more space. So big shopping malls are often found there.

City streets have sidewalks and streetlights. Some of the streets may be "one way." This means you can only drive in one direction. It is **uncommon** to find these things in a suburb.

There are other differences, too. The people in the city can walk to many places. Children may walk to school. The people in the suburbs often must drive to get places. So most children in a suburb ride school buses.

City or Suburb?

Comprehension Questions

Fill in the circle next to the best answer.

1. Factories are often found in

   (a) cities.

   (b) suburbs.

   (c) the country.

2. What happens last?

   (a) Children ride.

   (b) Children get off at school.

   (c) Children get on a bus.

3. Why do the city homes have smaller yards than the ones in the suburbs?

   (a) No one in the city wants a big yard.

   (b) It costs too much to have a big yard in a city.

   (c) There isn't as much space in a city.

4. *Uncommon* means

   (a) rare.

   (b) not funny.

   (c) not sad.

5. The people in a city can walk to many places because

   (a) they are rich.

   (b) many things are close by.

   (c) they are strong.

6. Picture a city street. What don't you see?

   (a) tall buildings

   (b) a parking lot

   (c) a cow grazing on grass

7. Where would you most like to live: in a city, in a suburb, or in the country? Explain.

_____

_____

_____

History Standard: Understands the history of a local community and how communities in North America varied long ago

Benchmark: Understands the daily life of a colonial community

Early American Colonies

When people first came from Europe to America, many families came together. They set up small towns called **colonies**. They built homes from logs. They used tree bark to cover their roofs. Their homes were cold when the wind blew. Their homes were wet when it rained. Each home had a fireplace for cooking, warmth, and light.

The people cut down trees to make beds, tables, and chairs. They had wooden cups and plates, too. They used shells for spoons. Each family had an iron pot. In it they made soup, candles, and soap.

To get food, the men hunted deer and turkey. They fished. Children picked wild berries. The people also planted crops. Everyone, even the children, had to work in the fields. If they did not, there would not be enough to eat.

Early American Colonies

Comprehension Questions

Fill in the circle next to the best answer.

1. **Who had to work in the fields?**

   (a) the children

   (b) everyone

   (c) the women

2. **What happened last?**

   (a) The people reached America.

   (b) The people in Europe wanted to come to America.

   (c) The people got on a ship.

3. **Why did the people use wood to make so many things?**

   (a) They didn't like metal.

   (b) They didn't have the money to buy things at the store.

   (c) There were lots of trees they could cut down.

4. **Another word for *colonies* is**

   (a) communities.

   (b) farms.

   (c) forts.

5. **Why were the homes wet when it rained and cold when the wind blew?**

   (a) There were small gaps between the logs in the walls.

   (b) The homes had no roofs.

   (c) The homes had too many windows.

6. **Picture an early American colony.   Look at the homes.   What does every home have?**

   (a) windows

   (b) a chimney

   (c) shutters

7. **Would you have liked being a child in an early American colony?   Explain.**

   _____

   _____

   _____

History Standard: Understands how democratic values came to be and how they have been exemplified by people, events, and symbols

Benchmark: Knows the history of American symbols

She Made the First American Flag

Betsy Ross made the first American flag. She had never made a flag before. But she was good at sewing. She sewed cloth onto chairs in her shop.

In June 1776 George Washington took a drawing to Betsy. He asked her to make a flag from the picture. The flag had seven red stripes. These stripes stood for bravery. The flag had six white stripes. These stripes stood for truth. The flag also had a blue square with a circle of 13 white stars. The blue stood for justice, or fairness. The flag had one star for each of the colonies.

Today's flag looks a lot like that first flag. The difference is the number of stars. Flag Day is June 14. On that day we **celebrate** our beautiful flag.

She Made the First American Flag

Comprehension Questions

Fill in the circle next to the best answer.

1. **How many stripes are on the American flag?**

   ⓐ 6

   ⓑ 7

   ⓒ 13

2. **What happened first?**

   ⓐ George Washington visited Betsy Ross.

   ⓑ June 14 was named Flag Day.

   ⓒ Betsy Ross sewed a flag.

3. **How many colonies were there when the first flag was made?**

   ⓐ 13

   ⓑ 7

   ⓒ 6

4. **Another word for *celebrate* is**

   ⓐ sew.

   ⓑ honor.

   ⓒ wash.

5. **Why aren't the stars in a circle on today's flag?**

   ⓐ Circles on flags are no longer in style.

   ⓑ Most people don't like circles.

   ⓒ There are so many states that the stars would have to be too tiny.

6. **Picture Betsy sewing the first flag. What is she using?**

   ⓐ a needle and thread

   ⓑ a sewing machine

   ⓒ fabric glue

7. **If you had chosen the colors for the first American flag, would you have used red, white, and blue? Explain.**

   _____

   _____

   _____

History Standard: Understands how democratic values came to be and how they have been exemplified by people, events, and symbols

Benchmark: Knows the history of American symbols

The American Bald Eagle

A symbol stands for something. The U.S. flag is a symbol of our country. When you see it, you think of America. The American bald eagle is another U.S. symbol. It was picked in 1782. This beautiful bird lives only in North America. It's strong, and it can live up to 50 years. That's quite a long time for a bird.

The American bald eagle is not bald. It has white feathers on its head. The rest of its feathers are brown. The food it likes best is **salmon**. So it lives near streams and rivers. That makes it easy to catch the fish.

A male and female will stay together for life. Each year they use the same nest. Each year they have one or two eggs. Taking care of their hungry babies is a lot of work. Both of the parents take turns finding food. When one goes hunting, the other watches over the nest.

The American Bald Eagle

Comprehension Questions

Fill in the circle next to the best answer.

1. **The American bald eagle is a symbol for**

   ⓐ South America.

   ⓑ North America.

   ⓒ the U.S.A.

2. **What happens last?**

   ⓐ The eagles pick mates.

   ⓑ The eagles take turns finding food.

   ⓒ One or two babies hatch.

3. **What is odd about the American bald eagle's name?**

   ⓐ It makes you think that eagle doesn't live a long time.

   ⓑ It makes you think the eagle's head is bald, but it isn't.

   ⓒ It makes you think that the eagle lives in North America.

4. ***Salmon* is a kind of**

   ⓐ mouse.

   ⓑ snake.

   ⓒ fish.

5. **Why is it important that the bald eagle can live for 50 years?**

   ⓐ The people who picked it as a symbol wanted America to last a long time, too.

   ⓑ We don't want to pick a new symbol more often than every 50 years.

   ⓒ The bird has to get old before it gets bald.

6. **Picture an eagle catching salmon. How does the eagle grab its prey?**

   ⓐ with its feet

   ⓑ with its wings

   ⓒ with its head

7. **Do you think the American bald eagle was a good choice for a symbol? Explain.**

   _____

   _____

   _____

History Standard: Understands how democratic values came to be and how they have been exemplified by people, events, and symbols

Benchmark: Knows why important buildings, statues, and monuments are associated with state and national history

The Statue That Stands for Freedom

The Statue of Liberty stands on an island near New York City. She has a crown. In one hand she has a light. In the other she has a book. The book has "July 4, 1776" on it.

In 1876 the people of France sent the statue as a gift to America. They put their gift into 214 big boxes on a ship. The ship ran into a bad storm. It almost went down.

At last the ship reached America. But Lady Liberty is so big that it took two years to put her back together! Each one of her fingers is longer than a man is tall. Inside of her are stairs. Each year many people go up the stairs to her crown. At night her crown and **torch** glow with light. Day or night, she is a beautiful sight.

The Statue That Stands for Freedom

Comprehension Questions

Fill in the circle next to the best answer.

1. **The Statue of Liberty is near**

   ⓐ New York City.

   ⓑ France.

   ⓒ Washington, D.C.

2. **What happened last?**

   ⓐ The ship nearly went down.

   ⓑ It took two years to put the Statue of Liberty together.

   ⓒ The French people sent America a gift.

3. **Think about the size of the Statue of Liberty's fingers. Next to them you would be**

   ⓐ taller.

   ⓑ larger.

   ⓒ smaller.

4. **Another word for *torch* is**

   ⓐ book.

   ⓑ light.

   ⓒ face.

5. **Why do you think that the French people gave America the gift in 1876?**

   ⓐ It was America's 100th birthday.

   ⓑ America had just won the war to be free of British rule.

   ⓒ France had just become a part of America.

6. **Picture looking out from the Statue of Liberty's crown. The people on the ground below look**

   ⓐ huge.

   ⓑ small.

   ⓒ normal size.

7. **Would you like to visit the Statue of Liberty? Explain.**

   _____

   _____

   _____

History Standard: Understands how democratic values came to be and how they have been exemplified by people, events, and symbols

Benchmark: Understands the reasons that Americans celebrate national holidays

Presidents' Day

Over 200 years ago Americans had to fight to be free from British rule. George Washington led the fight and won. Then he led America for another eight years as the first president. We call him the Father of our Country. Our country's capital is named for him.

Abe Lincoln was another president. He did not want people to have **slaves**. He said that one person could not own another. The people in the North said that Lincoln was right. The people in the South said that he was not. This led to the Civil War. The men from the North fought the men from the South. When the war ended, everyone was free.

Both leaders believed in freedom. Both had to fight a war to make people free. Both were born in February. Now a day in February honors them. We call it Presidents' Day.

Presidents' Day

Comprehension Questions

Fill in the circle next to the best answer.

1. Who did George Washington fight?

ⓐ the British

ⓑ Abe Lincoln

ⓒ the Mexicans

2. What happened first?

ⓐ George Washington was president.

ⓑ Abe Lincoln was president.

ⓒ The Northern states and Southern states fought each other.

3. After the Civil War

ⓐ people started to own slaves.

ⓑ all slaves were free.

ⓒ American had to fight the British.

4. What are *slaves*?

ⓐ people who fight

ⓑ people who do work

ⓒ people who belong to another person

5. The capital of the United States of America is

ⓐ Washington, D.C.

ⓑ Philadelphia.

ⓒ Boston.

6. Picture the month of February on the calendar. It has

ⓐ all odd numbers for its dates.

ⓑ more days than any other month.

ⓒ fewer days than any other month.

7. Do you think that it's fair that Washington and Lincoln are the only presidents that have a holiday? Explain.

_____

_____

_____

History Standard: Understands how democratic values came to be and how they have been exemplified by people, events, and symbols

Benchmark: Understands the reasons that Americans celebrate national holidays

Memorial Day

In 1866 some women showed that they cared about the **soldiers** who had died in the Civil War. They put flowers on their graves. They did it for men from both sides. They wanted to honor them all. Newspapers wrote about their kind act.

People thought it was a good idea. So a day was set aside to do this. We call it Memorial Day. It is on the last Monday of May each year. On this day we think of all of the men and women who have fought for America. We think of those who fought in the Civil War and all of the wars before and since. Many of them gave their lives for our country. It is a day to think about how happy we are to be free.

We get Memorial Day off from school. There are parades and speeches. Flowers or flags are put on graves.